SUNRISE THROUGH ASHES

Albert C. Ellis Sr.

ISBN 979-8-88644-047-8 (Paperback)
ISBN 979-8-88644-048-5 (Digital)

Covenant Books
11661 Hwy 707
Murrells Inlet, SC 29576
www.covenantbooks.com

This book is dedicated to my granny,
"Big Mama" Nellie C. Wilson.

Chapter 1

BLINDNESS

Blindness is in everything that anyone has gone or will be going through in their personal life—good or bad, spiritual or natural. Then, at some point, there is one life-changing event. One must consider what is important and what matters most, because there will be a mixture of light and darkness inside everyone's journey through life. So ponder on what's good, learn from what's bad, seek out the spiritual, and learn as much from the natural. Then, make a decision to follow the spirit of truth in the true light of Jesus Christ! Jesus said, "I am the Light that has come into the world" (John 8:12), and darkness comprehended it not. From the throne of grace to your heart, receive Jesus today. Today is the day of salvation!

Now, after you receive Jesus Christ as your personal Savior, you begin a new journey in life. This brings new awareness and a strong desire to seek out the church, one that teaches both the Old and New Testaments but also gives altar calls after each sermon to allow a soul whose heart has been touched by the sermon, through the Holy Spirit. Once you're involved in this type of ministry, you must observe and take part in learning as much as you can from each sermon until you see a significant change in your life. Also, there must be a diligent study of the Word of God personally. One must start in the beginning, Genesis. Read, read, and read. Try not to understand—just read.

Through reading, the Holy Spirit of God Almighty will overshadow you with insight that man or woman can't teach or instruct. This journey in your "new life" will be driven by the Holy Spirit.

Now, once this awakening starts to take place, you will be so amazed at your new life in Jesus Christ. After a while of going to church, you'll be led to do many things hands-on as the Holy Spirit leads you. This insight will be so amazing to all that you ever thought could be achieved. Never stop your reading of God's Word. Also, one must study, study, and study each story, each Psalm, each Proverb, each letter, and the book of Revelation. But heed what Jesus spoke more personally because a relationship with Jesus is so important.

Just going to church is not enough. It's easy to get caught up in the act of repetitiveness (where you're involved), but in reality one's awareness of truth is blinded to the point that one is seeing but not truly hearing. The natural man or woman cannot or will not receive anything from God Almighty, because things and promises from the throne of God Almighty are spiritual and they who worship must worship in the spirit of truth in Jesus Christ (John 4:23). There are many roads that lead to a dead end and many roads that lead to church. If that is the focus, what's the purpose? So many people don't know.

One may say, "Purpose?" What's purpose got to do with anything when you truly focus on what matters most in the natural mindset? Because what one believes is so relevant to their success or ministry.

Therefore, anything that comes against what one believes is a problem, offense, foolishness, or just not true. In today's society it's easier to believe a lie than truth, unrighteousness than righteousness, or religion than sound doctrine. Through my research overtime, I've come to understand that true religion is taking care of orphans and widows. But as far as the world's view, it's many views and channels of thought. So, through my search in the worldview, I've come to believe that religion according to the world is man or woman attempting to reach God themselves (or to rule hell doesn't exist). Therefore, I come to this understanding.

Then this revelation came to me from the throne of heaven saying, "I am Spirit. They who worship Me must worship Me in spirit and truth because I am Spirit, not a man who lies. I gave the world meaning. Father God Almighty gave His only begotten Son. And whosoever shall believe in Him, Jesus, shall not die but have eternal life" (John 3:16). It's not the fact that we can go to God. But the thought in truth is He first came to us, then showed Himself to us, walked with us, ate with us, worked miracles around us and through us, fed us, and then died for us. And the world thinks it is just about a book that men wrote and most of it—if not all of it—is fiction to one's imagination. To us believers it's more than just fiction. It's fact upon fact beyond all beliefs!

Chapter 2

LIGHT SHINES IN DARKNESS

One day, back in the 1970s, my great-grandma, Nelie C. Wilson, who was born on October 5, 1896, in Jackson, Mississippi, was talking to me about my parents because I would always ask.

"Well, come here, child. Your father was Claude Red Gilmore. They called him 'Photo Red,' and he worked for the Bill Haines Carnival as their photographer. Your mother was my only grand-daughter, whom I raised. Her name was Ardis Loraine Ellis."

And then I asked, "What happened to them?"

She said, "Well, Red had already had a family and was trying to take you from us, but I wouldn't let him. So, after a while, I never saw him again. And one day your mother said, 'Big Momma, I need you to watch Red for me, okay? I'll be right back.'"

"I'll be right back" turned into years. Now, Mrs. Wilson was well up in age, being that she was born in 1896 on a Jackson, Mississippi, plantation. While surely slavery was but not on that plantation, Mrs. Wilson described to me the difference between "house niggers" and "field niggers." House niggers were treated like freed slaves, while field niggers were treated as though slavery wasn't over—even though slavery was over at that time in the early 1900s. But just like slave mentality or prison mentality, some of us are still blinded through the darkness of our past, like when Moses tried to lead the children of Israel out the wilderness and they said, "It was better for us in the hand of Pharaoh" (Exodus 14:12). In fact, they said even further, "You brought us out here to *die*!" Unbelievable!

They had seen all the miracles of Father God Almighty at that time to deliver them from the hand of Satan. What has Father God Almighty done in your life that you can't deny to the point that you would rather be in darkness than follow the light of righteousness? No matter what, true light always shines in darkness so that whosoever is lost can find their way home, just like the prodigal son (Luke 15:11–32). One day this son asked his father for his inheritance, being that his father was a wealthy man. Now, he was still alive, so he gave his son a portion of his inheritance. Then, the son left his father's estate, went out making friends, partied, partied, and partied. After a while, when his money ran out, he lost all his friends and had no money to continue his party time. So he wandered around, down and out. He was in despair, hungry, thirsty, and—most importantly—hopeless! Then, after wandering around, he found a job feeding pigs—the lowest position on the employment scale. He was so hungry while feeding the pigs his mind started pondering on his father and his father's servants to the point that he realized his father's servants ate better than these pigs! Almost at the point of eating the pigs' slop, he came to himself and said, "If I go back to my father's house and become a servant, I'll be treated better than this!" Now, still hungry and thirsty, he quit his job immediately and started walking back home. The amazing point in this prodigal son's life is the fact that every day after the father allowed his son to leave, the father stood and looked from his gates daily for his son's return.

Then, one day, down the road, the father saw what he thought was his son. He went and told all his servants, "Go and prepare meats. Dress the table, for my son who was lost is coming back home!" Then, he went out to the front gates to take a closer look, hoping it really was his son. Without a second thought, the prodigal son's father started running toward him.

There comes a time in the life of every son or daughter of Father God Almighty that they may feel like the young man in this story. I'll go a little further. Let's say you're an alcoholic, a substance abuser, addicted to inappropriate websites, or just demon-possessed. There is still hope! The world says, "Never say never." And I say, "*Never* give up." In any situation that you're facing in life, consider the prodigal son when he started pondering. Remember he was hungry, thirsty, dirty, and at a defining moment in his life. Doing the same thing over and over again expecting to gain different results is insanity. So you may be at your last drink, drug, or website search. But until you truly come to your senses, nothing miraculous will happen in your personal life. You truly have to be sick and tired. I mean truly *sick* and *tired* of doing things your way. Period!

The woman with the issue of blood was at that point also. Just think about this. A woman with a flow of blood for twelve years lost all her money on seeing doctors and lost all her friends because of her condition. In addition, at that time in history, one would be considered "unclean" or a "cast-out." One day, she heard that Jesus was coming by her way. This is a point in Jesus's ministry where He was helping close friends of His inner circle. Jairus, a good friend, had gone to find Jesus because his daughter was very sick and he knew Jesus could heal her. After a while, he found Jesus and told Him what had happened to his daughter. So Jesus and Jairus started walking back to Jairus's house, but in the journey they passed many villages. Word got out that Jesus was passing through: "If you need a miracle, Jesus the Worker is passing by." Then, the woman with the issue of blood said to herself, "If I may but touch the hem of his garment, I shall be whole" (Matthew 9:21 KJV). As she was unclean, she dressed herself with more than enough clothing to keep as much blood covered so the crowd would not notice her condition. She even went a step further when she knew Jesus was close enough to her. She started crawling toward Him, by faith, reaching up as she crawled toward Jesus. Now, the crowd at this time was so large that they were stepping on her while she was crawling. Then she touched the hem of Jesus's garment, His robe, and immediately her blood flow dried up!

Then Jesus said, "Who touched Me?"

The disciples said, "Master, look at the crowd."

Jesus replied, "No! I felt virtue come from Me." Then he turned and said, "Woman, thy faith has made thee whole" (Matthew 9:22).

Basically, when you come to your senses from pondering on good things, the second step is faith. Faith without works is dead (James 2:26), and furthermore, "Faith is the substance of things hoped for, the evidence of things not seen" (Hebrews 11:1 KJV).

FROM BLINDNESS TO SEEING

In the early to late 1980s, one was till blind, but not blind according to the natural. Then, something started to happen in the early 1990s. A great light began to shine in one's dark place, like when Jesus met the demon-possessed man from the country of the Gerasenes, which was opposite Galilee. Most times, in today's world, we may judge one's behavior as evil or what one has done in the past as evil and the person is doomed to darkness, not realizing the person is demon-possessed. Jesus got off the boat, made it to land, and then met this man (one must read Luke 8:30). This man had two thousand demons inside of him, but he didn't cry out first. The demons cried out at the feet of Jesus through the man's person. Jesus had to cast the demons out first before the man could be in his right mind. So one began to think how powerful the presence of God is. The very presence of Jesus made the demons demand to be cast out of the man whom they had possessed for a long time. So now I hope you can see how powerful the true light of Jesus Christ is! Demons have to flee, diseases have to flee, generational curses have to flee, addictions have to flee, and any satanic attacks have to flee. There is power in His presence but more *power* in His *name*! In the name of Jesus, the eyes of the blind will be opened, and the ears of the deaf shall be unstopped. So, after you "see spiritually," you can "hear spiritually" as well. In the beginning, the spirit of God Almighty hovered over the face of the deep or moved upon the waters (Genesis 1:2). So, over many years, one researched, studied, and pondered to the extreme, only to be left with no true revelation because one knew that God Almighty gave

Joseph divine revelation to interpret Pharaoh's dreams. He also gave divine revelation through their journey in their personal life. So, one day, in deep study in the spirit of truth in Jesus Christ, one asked the Father in Jesus's name to help them understand the back office of the Holy Bible. One said, boldly, "Father God Almighty, You're not a respecter of persons, and I believe Your Holy Word from Genesis through Revelation. And, Father, speaking of the book of Revelation in which You took John in the spirit, by Your only begotten Son, Jesus Christ, and then revealed to John what must take place in the end of days, now!"

John was a man just like one. Then, as one was consulting the Father of all creation, Abba, one called to Him in His presence. He or she who is reading this epistle must ponder this truth: Jesus said, "I am the way, the truth and the life: no man cometh unto the Father, but by me" (John 14:6 KJV). So, further, one knew one had to walk with Jesus many years to understand that Jesus is the Christ! Therefore, one can ask anything in His name according to Father God Almighty's will. Then, one's brain was overwhelmed with divine revelation from Genesis through the book of Revelation. One could see all the people of faith in a personal way, meaning unbelievable truth.

While one was in Abba Father's presence, one saw as Abba Father sees the spirit world or, as one likes to say, "in His presence." While in His glory, in this realm, one sweat great drops of blood, asking, "If it be possible, let this cup pass from me" (Matthew 26:39). We all must understand that this is a defining moment or turning point to understanding that Father God Almighty sets His will in motion. Once it's set, God's will must manifest to completion or a finish (John 19:30).

Chapter 4

THE BATTLE WITH TWO WILLS

Through life's journey, we must realize that it's not bipolar when we see someone go from zero to one hundred in a negative way and then thirty minutes later zero to one hundred in a positive way. It's light and darkness, or should I say that "every soul has two wills." These two wills constantly battle against one another. One will love one and hate the other or cleave to one and despise the other. It's clear: you can't have two masters! Ponder this: one wants to do God's will, but one not only does what's not pleasing to God but practices it, at the same time wanting to please God. It's a place where two can be in a house but divided. So, if a house is divided against itself, it cannot stand in peace or perform God's will to completion. Therefore, Jesus clearly gives us the breakthrough because He battled with two wills Himself. He was 100 percent human and 100 percent God. When Jesus asked the question of His only begotten Father Almighty God, Jesus said, "If it be possible, let this cup pass." Then, shortly after, Jesus said, "Nevertheless, let not my will be done but let thine will be done" (Luke 22:42). So the revelational key is "self-awareness consultation." You must make a decision no matter what. Ponder: Jesus had to do it through intense agony, sweating great drops of sweat as if it was blood. One will not be victorious in life's journey without making a decision to do God's will.

Chapter 5

In the World but Not of the World

In the beginning was the Word, and the Word was with God the Father. Then the Word became flesh and dwelt among us. "Jesus" is that Word! Therefore, in the beginning was Jesus, and Jesus was with God the Father. Then, Jesus became flesh and dwelt among us. One said, "In sundry times, who will for us?" Then there was silence in all of heaven. After the great war between Michael the archangel who defended heaven and every angel who obeyed God the Father's will and Satan, Satan became Michael's and the host of the heaven's enemy, including the throne of Father God Almighty and His only begotten Son, Jesus Christ. Satan convinced one-third of the army of Father God Almighty to disobey His will, so a great war broke out in heaven. But before the great war, Satan was created as Lucifer. Perfect was he created. Ponder: to every angel who was created, Father God Almighty gave a *personal name*—Michael, Warrior; Gabriel, Messenger; Lucifer, Worshipper. Lucifer was created as an orchestra within himself, meaning Lucifer was created to usher in worship that led *all* of Father God Almighty's creation to worship Him in spirit and truth.

So what happened to make Lucifer Satan? Well, it's simple. Father God Almighty created all angels with free will to choose by personal relationship to worship Him through obedience to Who He was. So, with Lucifer, his will got in the way to the point he caused a division among the angels of heaven. Lucifer brought worship to himself and then thought that with one-third of the angels on his side, he could take over heaven and Father God's throne. Ponder: One may be in a position of bringing in worship at a local church. After a while, one can get caught up in being important to the point that the congregation comes to hear the choir instead of the man or woman of Father God Almighty. Everything in the Bible is for our reproofing, correction, and instruction in righteous living and to give Father God Almighty all honor, worship, and praise out of a pure heart. So Michael and his angels fought against Satan and his angels. In the end, there was no more room or place for Lucifer/Satan and one-third of the angels of Father God Almighty. Satan fell like lightning from heaven to earth, and his angels followed.

Chapter 6

PURPOSE OF DARKNESS

The purpose of darkness is to bring fear where there is no light. Satan is darkness, and there is no light in him. He comes to seek out the true light in believers in Jesus Christ. Then, he kills and destroys their seed. Satan's purpose was to kill and destroy man who was made in Father God Almighty's image. So, just like in heaven, he started deceiving, but not through the head, through the weakest vessel, not through the leader, but the helper—the woman. Before the woman was taken out of the first man, Adam, Satan couldn't deceive, kill, or destroy Adam. Adam had total dominion over Satan, being of the earth, meaning dirt. Man in his natural state has no power within himself to defeat Satan. In man's natural state, his thoughts and the knowledge of his thoughts are good to bad, from birth to death. Only because for a divine reason did Father God Almighty create a tree of knowledge of good and evil in the garden of Eden. Also, He created a tree of the spirit of life in the midst of the garden. Why? Glad you asked! The tree of life represents Father God Almighty's spirit in truth with seeds of righteousness within itself. The tree of knowledge of good and evil represents mankind—male and female. In their fallen state of being impaired through a false sense of vision, wherever good and evil reside together, it can produce a force within itself for the purpose of giving energy for a limited time. It can also recharge itself through a period of rest. But in total reality of truth, to master knowledge of good and evil, the ultimate outcome is self-destruction and death is the reward. What choice or decision will you make today? Tired of hearing but not *truly hearing?* Tire of doing *your will?* Okay! Seek the spirit of life, because if not, darkness is at the door of your heart.

Chapter 7

PURPOSE OF LIGHT

The *purpose of light* was to give light upon the earth. Back in time, eve and morning was considered a day. Men could only work in light. That light was the sun. When night came, the moon shone less light but not enough for work—but for evildoers. People of Father God Almighty were of the day (light). One said it, and I'll say it again and again! Father God Almighty created two great lights: one to rule the day and one to rule the night. Everything that was created on the earth, under the sea, and above—the sun, the moon, and the stars— we can see with a naked eye. Why? Because what was created was not created by what we see. That's the mystery and true light of Father God Almighty. Abba Father is *light*, and in Him is no darkness!

This whole earth moans and groans for the manifestation of the Son of Father God Almighty! Abba Father shines His glorious *light* through man whom He created in His image. But the first light went dim, meaning Adam who listened or harkened to the voice of Eve instead of the voice of Father God Almighty in the garden in the cool of the day or morning. So weeping may endure through the night, but *joy* comes in the morning!

Therefore, the first Adam or man of Father God Almighty harkened to the voice of his wife, which led to the fall of mankind through the darkness of deception. Listen! Ponder with your whole heart: Who is the third voice in your mind—marriage, ministry, or personal life? Influence is one door to many roads of failure or success. Failure or success is not the key to one's purpose. If one had divine purpose and had died, no matter what happened, his or her seed would carry out the divine purpose—*redemption*, Father God Almighty's master plan. He sent His best *light* into the world—*Christ Jesus*—Who only listened to His Father's *voice* till death (John 3:16).

Albert C. Ellis Sr. was born to Ardis Loraine Ellis and an unknown father. He was raised by Nellie C. Wilson, his great grandma.

At two years old, Albert's granny decided to raise him after his mother dropped him off many times. At seventy, she had no choice. Albert remembers being pulled in a little red-and-black wagon to town by Granny, riding back with groceries around him. As he looks back on his early childhood, he is very thankful that his granny took him to church that was right down the street, about three houses down. She trained him up in the Lord Jesus Christ as best she could. She was very spiritual. She told him these words one day when he was very hungry, "Child, come here. Listen. When you grow up and have a house of your own, pay your rent if you can't pay for anything else, because a roof over your head is the most important thing as you get older."

Albert remembers one day at the age of four when it was raining very hard and he had to go to pre-K school. His granny put a yellow raincoat on him, the pants first and then the jacket. She then opened the side door and took his hands. As they walked outside, she stooped down, looked at him, and then said, "Don't worry about the rain. You get to school." Then she stepped back and let his hand go to shut the door. Albert was very scared as it seemed the rain started coming down very hard. He had no choice but to run, so he ran down the street. Two blocks away was an awning. So he ran very fast toward the awning. Once underneath, it seemed like his heart was about to come out of his chest. Then, as he caught his breath, he reached in his raincoat pocket because his granny had put his lunch inside, a sandwich, apple, and banana in a brown paper sack. But the top of the sack was saggy from the rain. Looking to the corner as he got ready to run again, coming up the street in the rain was the neighborhood bum, riding his bike. So Albert thought quickly to run toward him and give him his lunch. Albert remembers him smiling at him while taking his lunch. Then the rain started to lighten up. Immediately the bum rode off, and Albert ran to school eight blocks away happily!

As Albert looks back, Father God was with him as his granny prayed for him. He knows now that it was her personal relationship with Jesus Christ that helped her raise him. So much more to share, but let's move forward to her funeral. The woman who meant the world to Albert was gone. He remembers riding in a black vehicle to a cemetery that had so many tombstones. They drove up the side, then turned left, drove further down the hill, turned left again, and went down the side of the cemetery to the very bottom. Albert remembers sitting and looking at his granny in the coffin. He kept feeling people touch his shoulder and then saying, "Mrs. Nellie was a good woman" or "Your grandma was a precious woman." As he turned around, Albert couldn't see any tombstones because there were so many people who covered the whole cemetery. He remembers a man taking his hand, asking him to say something to his granny. He walked to the casket and looked at her. She was so beautiful, and she was smiling. Then he reached in and kissed her and told her he loved her and missed her so much! After the funeral, Albert does not remember much, but he does remember going from house to house with other families.

As a young man, Albert was suicidal, confused, and demon-possessed, contemplating his death because he didn't want to live anymore. He was fighting something in him that made him do things he didn't want to do but would do, which he would later hate. So, one time after working a third shift at a food warehouse, he planned to take his own life. But he didn't want to use a gun, a knife, or a rope. So he decided to drive off a bridge that he crossed over the nights he drove to work. It basically was on overpass. He said to himself, "Everyone will think it's an accident from working late and then being sleepy." So, as Albert was driving to the spot, he grabbed the steering wheel, making a hard turn to the left, but then realized his house was thirty miles away. Immediately he thought he was dreaming. So he kept driving, passing by his house, getting back on the highway just driving reflecting on his day as if it was a dream. Then very tired, he took the first exit, pulled into a parking lot, and fell asleep. Then suddenly it seemed that there was a loud knock at his driver's window. He thought it was the police, but it was a preacher. He pulled into a church parking lot. Albert opened the door.

The preacher said, "God bless you, son. You're in the right place. Come with me." They walked around to the front when immediately the parking lot was filling up with cars. People came from every direction. Then the pastor said to someone, "Show him in." Then he was gone. Albert remembers walking with all the people. They were so happy once inside, sitting down. The pastor addressed the crowd, which must have been about five hundred people, with a question. He said, "Does anyone know him?" And everyone knew him except Albert for what he had done. Then quickly the pastor said he committed suicide behind his mother's house Friday night. Then there was silence, as if you could hear a pin drop. He kept ministering, as if he was talking directly to Albert. Tears flowed down Albert's face. Then he remembers the pastor say, "There may be one in here right now, and if you are listening to the words that are coming out of my mouth, I want you to move quickly out into the aisle and come meet my Jesus. Come now!" Albert is so glad he did!